John Honeyman

HUMBLE PATRIOT

(A STORY BASED ON ACTUAL EVENTS)

Family History StoryBooks

In the heart of colonial America, amidst the turmoil of the Revolutionary War, lived a man named John Honeyman. To the world, he was a humble butcher and weaver, but behind closed doors, he led a double life—one that would forever alter the course of history.

Honeyman had come to America from Ireland in the mid 1700's as a soldier in the British Army. Though he received no formal education, he learned quickly and soon earned the respect of his British generals.

When his Army tour was over, he moved to Philadelphia. Here he met two people who would change the course of his life forever. The first was General George Washington who would entrust Honeyman with a key role in saving his new country. The second was a kind-hearted woman named Mary, whose Irish roots matched his.

John and Mary were married in 1764. Together, they built a cozy home, nestled among the green fields of New Jersey. John established a successful business as a weaver and a butcher. Mary took care of their expanding family.

Soon the sounds of little feet echoed through their house—including their eldest daughter, Jane, who found walking difficult because of her club feet. Altogether, they would have seven children. It is from their fifth child, Eleanor, that your great grandfather Max Porter Reid is descended.

In the next few years, contentions began to rise between the American colonists and the King of Great Britain. Even though John had come to America as a British soldier, he knew he wanted to help his new land. He also understood that he was in a unique situation to assist because of his military experience and knowledge of people.

Late one evening, he and Mary came to an important decision. John would use his brave heart and clever mind to become a spy—feeding false information to the British while secretly aiding the American Revolution. It was a dangerous choice but one that would help secure a brighter future for their children.

Soon after, John set out for Philadelphia to meet once more with George Washington, who had now become the Commander of the Continental army. With a firm handshake and a hopeful heart, John offered his skills as a spy. Washington saw the sincerity in John's eyes and knew he had found a loyal friend.

Together, they plotted quietly, crafting plans that would hopefully lead to American independence. John would pretend to be a Tory, a loyal supporter of the British. It was the perfect disguise for gathering whispers and secrets from the new enemy. He would wear the mask of a British loyalist, but his heart would beat true for the cause of freedom.

With a letter from George Washington promising the safety of his young family, John left home to spin his silent secrets, watched over by the trusting eyes of his new friend.

Under the cover of darkness, he met with fellow spies in dimly lit taverns. They exchanged coded messages, hidden in loaves of bread or stitched into the lining of coats. John's heart raced as he passed along tidbits—the British troop movements, their weaknesses, their plans.

By the chilly winds of mid-November 1776, John had reinvented himself a butcher and cattle dealer, mingling with the British forces as if he were one of their own. With a friendly smile and a cart full of goods, he moved among the soldiers, his ears open to their careless talk of war plans.

As he sold them meat, he stole their secrets, collecting the classified intelligence for General Washington. All the while, John wore his Tory guise like a well-fitted coat, keeping his true allegiance hidden under the cover of everyday trades.

Mary was fearful of John being found out, so she played into the Tory act, just like her husband. The safety of their children weighed heavily on both their minds.

As the Christmas of 1776 approached, John Honeyman had the perfect Christmas present for George Washington- information about the location of a critical encampment of troops- but he needed to reach the Commander-in-Chief without raising suspicion.

It was exhausting to live a double life. Every fiber of his being wanted independence and freedom from the tyrannical rule of the King who was abusing power and American resources.

With fiery passion for such a noble cause, John felt a sense of conflict every day he had to feign loyalty to Great Britain. He knew that if his neighbors or associates found out he was conspiring for the revolution, his work as a spy would be for naught. So John came up with a plan to get himself captured by continental soldiers.

After much searching in continental territory, John finally found two American soldiers resting with their horses. Nearby, he spied a cow, grazing on a clump of grass poking through the newly fallen snow. Sneaking up to the cow, John nudged her towards the resting men.

Startled, she started to run, and John jumped and shouted after her, pretending to steal her as part of his job as a cattle dealer. Glancing up to see what all the shouting was about, the two continental soldiers thought that an enemy cattle dealer was trying to steal a local farmer's cow.

They jumped onto their horses and quickly overtook John, tackling him to the ground. He wrestled against their attempts to bind him and pleaded with them to release him, but they treated him roughly and dragged him through the dirt all the way back to camp.

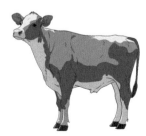

He was eventually brought before General Washington. Despite the ropes that bound his wrists, John's spirit soared with joy, ready to deliver his special Christmas gift: crucial enemy information that could turn the tide of the war.

When the General saw whom his soldiers had dragged in, he ordered them to stand guard at the door outside. He also told them they were to shoot-to-kill if the prisoner tried to escape. Once the guards left, George clasped John's hand and smiled. John told him about the Hessian troops he had been living with in Trenton.

These soldiers, hired from Germany to fight for the British, were busy with Christmas celebrations, thus paying little attention to their defenses. They didn't realize their merrymaking would leave them terribly unprepared for what could come.

As John shared the secrets of the distracted Hessians, his words painted a picture of opportunity in the air. The Hessians, enjoying their festivities, had let their guard down. This was the chance Washington had been hoping for—a chance to strike when least expected. This intelligence was just what the Americans needed.

George Washington, eager to begin planning his own Christmas surprise for the Trenton Hessians, humbly thanked John. Resuming a stoic expression, he called the guards back in. As a prisoner, John Honeyman was to be locked up in the guardhouse.

It was a long and cold night for John. He missed his family. His heart and body ached from being treated so poorly by the soldiers who should have been his allies, but he knew his sacrifices were helping achieve the liberty of a new nation.

Early the next morning, a haystack nearby suddenly caught fire! The guard who was charged with John's imprisonment ran from his post to help extinguish the fire before it spread to General Washington's headquarters. When he returned to the guardhouse, he gaped in disbelief at the door which had been mysteriously unlocked, making it possible for John to escape.

John scrambled over slippery ice and waded through the frigid, bone-chilling water of the Delaware River. Soaked and shivering, he reached the New Jersey side. Exhaustion almost overcame him as he stumbled into a Hessian outpost, but his mission was not yet over.

In the British Colonel's quarters, John spun the tale of his capture and escape. To Colonel Rall, he portrayed himself as a loyal British subject who had revealed nothing to Washington. He told the Colonel of disarray among the American troops, suggesting they were on the verge of mutiny, struggling to stay united. Delighted, Colonel Rall took the bait, seeing no reason to halt his Christmas festivities.

After relaying this inaccurate story to Colonel Rall, John knew he needed to get away from Trenton before George Washington's strike. So, he returned to his home and collapsed into his wife's welcoming arms.

Unfortunately, though, whispers of John Honeyman's escape spread like wildfire. American patriots thought they could aid George Washington by hunting down the fugitive Tory. With their torches flickering in the dark, they swarmed his home.

Inside, ten-year-old Jane clung to her mother's dress as fear ripped through her. Her heart pounded as voices outside threatened to burn their home to the ground if her father did not surrender.

But Mary stood firm at the door. With her children huddled about her skirts, she denied knowledge of John's whereabouts. However, she knew that the mob would not be satisfied until they found him, so she asked to speak to the leader of the mob.

When a soldier stepped forward, Mary carefully and privately unfolded a letter from General Washington declaring that the family was to be kept safe from harm.

Grudgingly, the soldier nodded as the group turned to leave. Relief washed over Mary as she closed the door. Her children were safe for another night.

On Christmas night, three days later, the continental troops gathered on the frozen shores of the Delaware River in the predawn darkness. Silently, they filed into boats and crept across the water toward the unsuspecting British stronghold in New Jersey. "Victory or Death" they silently cried.

The British were caught unprepared. The tide turned. In less than an hour, over 1,000 enemy men were captured. This was indeed the victory that tipped the entire Revolutionary War into the colonist's favor. John Honeyman's incredible sacrifice in wrestling with and maintaining a double identity was critical to this triumphant outcome.

For the remainder of the war, John served as George Washington's confidential aide. After the encounter his family had with the vengeful mob, he decided to distance himself from home as an added measure of safety for his dear Mary and their children.

Even from a distance, however, John's troubles were far from over. He was jailed on charges of high treason in New Jersey, with the looming threat of a death sentence. His neighbors even testified against him, describing his Tory-sympathizing behavior. All of his possessions were confiscated and sold.

While malice from those he was actively working to defend was frustrating to John, he knew his cause was greater than himself. Thankfully, George Washington did not forget his promise to protect John and his family. Each of John's charges was quietly dismissed or resolved.

When peace in the colonies finally came in 1783, General Washington officially cleared John Honeyman's name. In fully decorated uniform, the General himself strode up the road to John's house with a party of continental officers to personally thank John for his silent, indispensable service. The dark cloud of distrust that had hovered over the Honeyman family for years was finally lifted.

With sweet relief, John and Mary settled into family life together for good. They now had five daughters and two sons and loved each one very much. Having liberated their futures, John became a prosperous farmer, working the land hand-in-hand with his wife and children.

Having his family by his side was reward enough to John. For the remainder of his long life of 93 years, he never sought recognition or public acclaim for his incredible contributions to his country. He was with his family, he was happy, and he was free.

John Honeyman

HUMBLE PATRIOT

JUNE 20, 1729-AUGUST 18, 1822

My Relationship:

FamilySearch.org ID: LKKM-79D

Book Created for John's Great-Great-Great-Great Grandson, Malcolm Reid

Order More Copies at familyhistorystorybooks.com

Family History StoryBooks

Did You Like this Book?
Let us tell YOUR story!
Come visit us at familyhistorystorybooks.com and we can turn your own treasured stories into a children's book

SCAN ME

George Washington thanks John Honeyman

John Honeyman Headstone, Somerset County, New Jersey

Washington Crossing State Park, New Jersey

John Honeyman House, Griggstown, New Jersey

96633818R00024